How to Date a Skateboarder

First edition

Names: Heroux, Chantelle, author

Title: How to Date a Skateboarder / by Chantelle Heroux

Identifiers: ISBN 979-8-9888259-0-6 (hardcover)

Subjects: Humor

A percentage of this book benefits the youth skateboarding organization, Bridge To Skate. To learn more about their programs, visit their website at www.bridgetoskate.org

To everybody that has big dreams of dating a person
that uses a shoelace for a belt.

Chapter 1

Don't.

Chapter 2

Don't.

Chapter 3

Don't.

Chapter 4

Don't.

Chapter 5

Don't.

Chapter 6

Don't.

Chapter 7

Don't.

Chapter 8

Don't.

Chapter 9

Don't.

Chapter 10

Don't.

Chapter 11

Don't.

Chapter 12

Don't.

Chapter 13

Don't.

Chapter 14

Don't.

Chapter 15

Don't.

Chapter 16

Don't.

Chapter 17

Don't.

Chapter 18

Don't.

Chapter 19

Don't.

Chapter 20

Don't.

Chapter 21

Don't.

Chapter 22

Don't.

Chapter 23

Don't.

Chapter 24

Don't.

Chapter 25

Don't.

Chapter 26

Don't.

Chapter 27

Don't.

Chapter 28

Don't.

Chapter 29

Don't.

Chapter 30

Don't.

Chapter 31

Don't.

Chapter 32

Don't.

Chapter 33

Don't.

Chapter 34

Don't.

Chapter 35

Don't.

Chapter 36

Don't.

Chapter 37

Don't.

Chapter 38

Don't.

Chapter 39

Don't.

Chapter 40

Don't.

Chapter 41

Don't.

Chapter 42

Don't.

Chapter 43

Don't.

Chapter 44

Don't.

Chapter 45

Don't.

Chapter 46

Don't.

Chapter 47

Don't.

Chapter 48

Don't.

Chapter 49

Don't.

Chapter 50

Don't.

Chapter 51

Don't.

Chapter 52

Don't.

Chapter 53

Don't.

Chapter 54

Don't.

Chapter 55

Don't.

Chapter 56

Don't.

Chapter 57

Don't.

Chapter 58

Don't.

Chapter 59

Don't.

Chapter 60

Don't.

Chapter 61

Don't.

Chapter 62

Don't.

Chapter 63

Don't.

Chapter 64

Don't.

Chapter 65

Don't.

Chapter 66

Don't.

Chapter 67

Don't.

Chapter 68

Don't.

Chapter 69

Don't.

In conclusion, don't.